Gates of Savannah

Best Wishes

[signature]

Gates of Savannah
A Walking Tour

MERANA CADORETTE

Charleston · London
History
PRESS

Published by The History Press
Charleston, SC 29403
www.historypress.net

Cover image: Watercolor by Merana Cadorette.

First published 2007

Manufactured in the United Kingdom

ISBN 978.1.59629.294.9

Library of Congress Cataloging-in-Publication Data

Cadorette, Merana.
  Gates of Savannah : a walking tour / Merana Cadorette.
    p. cm.
  Includes bibliographical references and index.
  ISBN 978-1-59629-294-9 (alk. paper)
  1. Gates--Georgia--Savannah--Guidebooks. 2. Savannah (Ga.)--Tours.
I.
Title.
  NA8390.C33 2007
  721'.82--dc22
                          2007011835

I dedicate this work with grateful thanks to all who have supported and encouraged me through the years; among them: Mom, who always wanted to write; Lona, whose heart lives partly in Savannah; Lillian and Marie, who helped make us at home in Savannah; Jan and Jami, who kept me busy when I wasn't painting(!); my children; and most especially and with everlasting love, to my husband Dave. Deservedly so; this book was his idea.

Contents

Acknowledgements

The information presented was acquired from a variety of sources. I collected a wealth of data from posted historical markers and plaques, books, pamphlets and brochures. Most interesting and gratifying were the anecdotes and tidbits from individual owners, blacksmiths, curators and archivists. Among these are James Morton, Martha Summerell, John Duncan, Sally Cowart, Steve Berg, Virginia Maxwell, Cyndi Sommers, Mark Bradley, Colonel Richard O. Stewart (Retired), John Boyd Smith, Sister Frances Ann Cook, Sister Jude, Ivan Bailey and the Historic Savannah Foundation. If I have forgotten anyone, my sincerest apologies.

Thank you.

Introduction

Savannah has many beautiful sights and a fascinating history. The colony of Georgia was founded February 12, 1733, on this site by James Edward Oglethorpe and an intrepid band of forty families. Chippewa Square features a bronze sculpture of Oglethorpe by noted American artist Daniel Chester French mounted on a plinth, standing valiantly facing the river with his dress sword planted point down in a palmetto frond.

The following anecdote came from John Smith to explain the molasses-like slowness of change in Savannah. When Oglethorpe left for England on his last voyage across the Atlantic, he gathered all the colony's leaders and left them this order: "Everything looks great, keep it like this until I get back." However, Oglethorpe never returned.

Countless books have been written on the city by historians as well as past and present occupants. The architecture has a wonderful, lived-in appearance. Homes settle into the earth, losing the stark planes and geometry of newer construction. The environment of the historic area is scaled to people and pedestrians,

Introduction

rather than vehicles. Nature softens further, subtly streaking the walls into an earthen palette and eroding harsh edges of brickwork. Residents have trimmed and restrained the foliage just enough to accentuate their constructions rather than hide it. Hanging moss frames vistas, while the velvet carpet below tries to reclaim the brick back into primal clay. Unlike modern cities, you feel attuned with its past generations.

Savannah's irregular pavement does not encourage people to stride purposefully, eyes staring far off. Ignoble falls await the inattentive! No, it is best to amble slowly, watching the surroundings closely, so an errant flagstone or whipping crepe myrtle branch doesn't put you too painfully in your place.

Why gates? Gates are portals that admit us into unknown, secluded areas. Ranging from the mundane to the majestic, they bar our way while teasing us with glimpses of where we cannot tread. When first strolling alongside a shaded wall, I began noticing them. Suddenly I would see a patch of light and a peek into a small pocket of Eden. Or, between the sidewalk and a door, there was a gate to cause the unwelcome to pause, but not deterring the friend. I was charmed by the myriad metal patterns and designs. Who chose these gates and why? How long have they hung there through seasons and generations? They lead to and from front doors, side doors, gardens, garages, homes, shops and churches.

If you are following the locations of these gates on a map, you will find a pattern. Properties are entered from north to south, from up by the river and original settlement outward. When more than one location occurs on a street, they are then listed from west to east. I hope this makes the hunt easier.

I have had many other gates suggested to me. Some were similar to ones I had already chosen. Others often have too much detritus or too little greenery around them. Many more lovely gates are just a few streets away from these, and if you wander a bit from the area on the map you can search out your own favorites. I know of several more that I itch to paint someday. Comparing my paintings with the real gates, a factor such as lighting or season may be different, and the image may not be as satisfying. Life, light and art are all ephemeral, and this is just one artist's small attempt to share a few special moments with you.

This guide was not so much written as painted. I am an artist, not a wordsmith. The bits of gossip, facts and whimsy are erratic pieces that seeped into my head as background while wandering the city.

These are very intimate paintings, best enjoyed closely. Like a leisurely promenade about town, these are best savored slowly. Since modern society goes so rapidly and old-fashioned artists must compete with the age of sound bites and instant impressions, I would rather delicately detail my work so there is

Introduction

always a new spot or special color, of light and shadow area awaiting discovery by returning viewers. I want to create a place you'll want to visit again and again. Although the brushwork is very controlled, wet-on-wet areas abound in the greenery, walkways and stucco. I favor an impressionistic look in my flowers and foliage, but apply my medium in layers similar to the gesso or the old oil painting techniques. My painting style is a pastiche of art styles as the buildings of Savannah are in historic styles, blending the past with the present to achieve a uniqueness all our own.

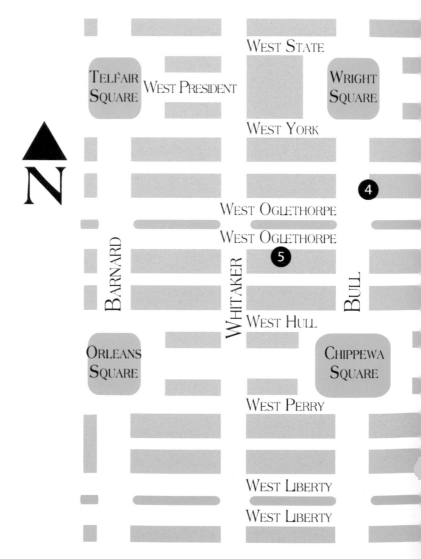

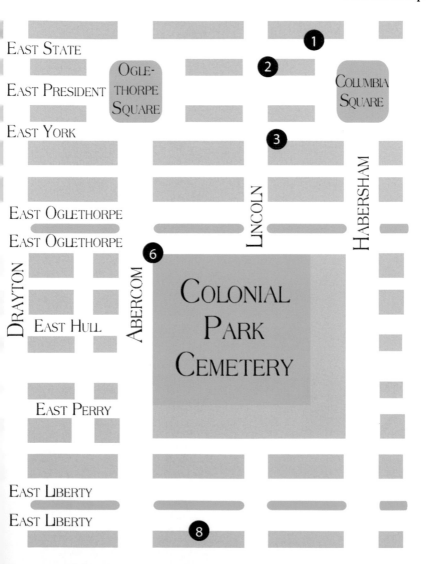

EAST STATE

OGLE-
THORPE
SQUARE

EAST PRESIDENT

COLUMBIA
SQUARE

EAST YORK

EAST OGLETHORPE

EAST OGLETHORPE

LINCOLN

HABERSHAM

DRAYTON

ABERCOM

EAST HULL

COLONIAL
PARK
CEMETERY

EAST PERRY

EAST LIBERTY

EAST LIBERTY

17

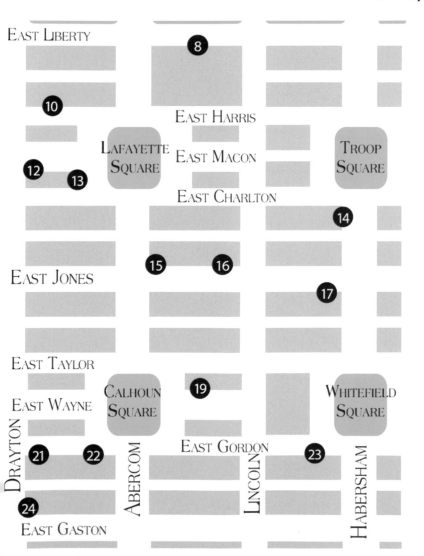

EAST LIBERTY

EAST HARRIS

LAFAYETTE SQUARE

EAST MACON

TROOP SQUARE

EAST CHARLTON

EAST JONES

EAST TAYLOR

CALHOUN SQUARE

EAST WAYNE

WHITEFIELD SQUARE

DRAYTON

ABERCOM

EAST GORDON

LINCOLN

HABERSHAM

EAST GASTON

1.

Davenport Garden Gate

Isaiah Davenport House
324 East State Street

Gates of Savannah

This property, the northernmost of my subjects, is among the oldest in the city. It is a Federal-style home completed by master builder Isaiah Davenport for his personal residence in 1820. Isaiah was a Rhode Islander who strayed South. Upon his death in 1827 of yellow fever, his wife, Sarah, transformed her home into a boardinghouse to feed her children.

She sold it for $9,000 in 1840 to William Baynard of Hilton Head, South Carolina. The Baynard family continued to own the Davenport House for over a century until 1955. During that period, it was rented as a single residence up to the 1920s, and then reverted back to a boardinghouse for multiple families as the Depression, then World War II, hit Savannah.

In 1955 the home and garden were purchased by Katherine Summerlin for demolition to make way for a parking lot to accommodate a funeral parlor. They were saved by the founding members of the Historic Savannah Foundation. Tour guides like to tell how the seven women (two of them were Girl Scouts—a board member and an interim director) chained themselves to the gates to halt its destruction. According to the Davenport museum director, however, this is sadly only a story.

This gate opens into the courtyard garden that was originated as a bicentennial project by the Trustees' Garden Club and was later redesigned by noted horticulturist Penelope Hobhouse.

2.

Owens-Thomas Museum Front Gate

124 Abercorn Street

Gates of Savannah

The Owens-Thomas House was designed by the young English Architect William Jay for merchant and banker Richard Richardson and his wife Frances Bolton. An inscription by master builder John Retan documents the construction: Begun Nov AD 1816 Finished Jan AD 1819.

The architecture of classical Greece and Rome and Regency England (1811–1820) influenced Jay's design. Richardson imported building materials and furnishings from England, and Jay brought with him the latest English technology as evidenced by the sophisticated plumbing system installed in the house and the cast-iron balcony on the south façade.

Richardson lost his new home after the financial panic of 1819. Its contents were sold in 1822 and the property reverted to the Bank of the United States. The house was rented to Mrs. Mary Maxwell, who ran it as a boardinghouse. Her most famous guest was the Revolutionary War hero, the Marquis de Lafayette, in 1825.

In 1830, lawyer George Welshman Owens and his wife, Sarah, bought the property for $10,000. Owens added three rooms to the upper story, which overlooked the garden. This is the only structural change made to Jay's original design. The property remained in the Owens family for 121 years. In 1951 Owens's granddaughter, Miss Margaret Thomas, bequeathed the site, which included the original 1819 urban slave quarters, to the Telfair Museum of Art. She requested it to be operated as a museum named for her grandfather and her father, Dr. James G. Thomas. On October 27, 1954, the Owens-Thomas House opened to the public.

These cast-iron gates, inscribed "D&W Rose Makers," were added to the property in the late 1800s. Probably manufactured for cemetery plots, the space at the top was left blank for the family name to be inserted.

This information was kindly provided for me by Cyndi Sommers, administrator, Telfair's Owens-Thomas House.

3.

Orange Tree Gate

Manse front on 134 Lincoln Street
Gate around the corner
on East York Street

Gates of Savannah

This Federal-style house was constructed in 1799 as the residence of William Barnard, nephew of Sir John Barnard, a distinguished patron of the Georgia colony. In 1808 William Barnard lost his wife, Sarah; his son-in-law, John Cooper; and a son to fever in Savannah.

The house was purchased in 1812 by the Methodist movement in Savannah as its first parsonage. The Reverend James Russell, first occupant of the parsonage, was responsible for the construction of Wesley Chapel, which stood just south of the property until its removal in 1954. It now serves as a Presbyterian manse.

The gate, by Ivan Bailey, leads into the attached garden. Bailey commented on the gate:

> *The Orange Tree gate was commissioned by a Reverend Jack Mummert who first asked for a St. Francis gate. I expressed more interest in a whole garden in one gate since the yard was nothing but a sinkhole at the time. He went for it. This gate had some pieces with fused enamel, red on the mushroom and blue on the cornflowers and copper fused onto the oranges. Clear finished, it was eventually painted. Once a branch, which did not fasten except in one place, was ripped off and the gate was sent to me to be restored. The man who owned the house at that time was the one who painted it black.*
>
> *I prefer not to be called an artist. Metalsmith or blacksmith is sufficient and goes better with my personal philosophy. I actually consider myself a toymaker for adults.*

4.

Wayne-Gordon House Side Gate

Museum and shop on the corner of
Bull and Oglethorpe Streets
Gate fronts on Bull Street

Gates of Savannah

While there are more famous gates created by Juliette Low herself, this anonymously made one has a simple elegance. It is very tall and narrow, giving the passerby a glimpse into the elegant back garden and sculptures inside. Currently, Girl Scout troops signed up for tours or programs enter here, making it a Girl Scout's first glimpse into where the organization's founder played as a child. The horse-head hitching post outside the gate patiently enjoys the attention of the eager girls awaiting admission.

The home was built in 1821 for Savannah Mayor James Moore Wayne, who was later an associate justice of the U.S. Supreme Court and founding member of the Georgia Historical Society. It showcases Egyptian Revival and classical details popular in the early 1800s. His niece, Sarah, and her husband, William Washington Gordon I (Juliette Low's grandfather), purchased it in 1831.

Juliette Gordon was born October 31, 1860, into a happy upper-middle-class family. The house was refurbished to reflect the Victorian era, with the added flavor of Southern charm.

A few ghosts roam the place, but, as can be expected for a house visited by hushed giggling girls, are all benevolent.

For a time in the early twentieth century, the home had gone from a family residence to subdivided apartments housing families of Savannah shipyard employees during World War II and was in desperate need of renovation.

The Gordon family sold the property in 1953, and it is currently owned and operated by the Girl Scouts of the United States of America as a program center, gift shop and house museum.

5.

Independent Presbyterian Church Courtyard Gate

Church and complex fill the entire block between
Oglethorpe, Bull and Whitaker Streets
Gate opens onto Oglethorpe

Gates of Savannah

The Independent Presbyterian Church complex courtyard gate fronts on Oglethorpe. One of the most formal looking properties in the city, it has been around since it was a humble kirk. The latter was erected on a site nearer the river granted by King George II and built by the first Scottish settlers less than twenty-five years after they first arrived with James Oglethorpe.

This rests upon the third site in Savannah to hold the Independent Presbyterian Church's congregation. Fires, ever-increasing membership and a hurricane have caused the church to move and rebuild their house of worship, but the foundation of the congregation remains intact. Many famous people have belonged to this church over the years, including President Woodrow Wilson, who was married here in 1885.

From the severe gray stone, through the manicured area past the fountain and up the curved stairs, this is regally set back and imposing in a city where most property sits close to (and sometimes abuts) the sidewalk. The edifice was originally designed by John Holden Green in 1817. A spectacular fire, which destroyed much of Savannah in 1889, created the need for a rebuilding, which was supervised by William G. Preston in 1891.

Colonel Richard O. Stewart (Retired), kirk archivist, passes on an interesting story:

> *There was a movie called* **A Man Named Mudd** [sic] *with Dennis Weaver, which was partially filmed here in Savannah a number of years ago. Mudd, as you may remember, was the doctor who treated President Lincoln's assassin. There is an unsubstantiated report that the scene where his* **(Mudd's)** *mother is looking through the gate at the White House is actually our gate and could be believable having seen* **(this)** *watercolor.*

6.

DAR Cemetery Gate

DAR gate Colonial Park Cemetery
on the corner of Oglethorpe and
Abercorn Streets

Gates of Savannah

With all the deaths in this city through the years from various diseases, piracy and slavery, it's no wonder this is often called the most haunted city in the United States. This DAR cemetery houses some of the local ghosts. It was founded in 1750 and used as a burial ground until the 1850s. It is the final resting spot for more than seven hundred victims of the 1820 yellow fever epidemic.

Conveniently enough, the city dueling grounds were located adjacent to the cemetery. One of the more famous duels led to the demise and burial of Button Gwinnett, a signer of the Declaration of Independence. His foe, General Lachlan McIntosh, survived and was interred next to him many years later.

During the War Between the States, General Sherman's army used the cemetery as a campground and snapped off several tombstones to make way for their tents, making the area a rather morbid place for soldiers to sleep.

The gate with the oversized eagle was erected in 1913 by the Daughters of the American Revolution in memory of the Patriots of the Revolutionary War. The park is no longer run by the DAR, and its grounds are now under the care of the City of Savannah.

7.

DeRenne Apartments Front Gate

Front entryway, DeRenne Apartments
24 Liberty Street

Gates of Savannah

In Savannah, there is an unwritten rule to reflect the original Oglethorpe city plans in new designs. In the early twentieth century, most Savannah architects followed the practice of breaking the mass of larger buildings into sixty-foot or smaller units. Thus, most of the city's older buildings have large footprints, but subdivide their fronts into false fronts or bays to unite them with established structures. The DeRenne Apartment Building, constructed in 1919, appears more like two buildings due to deep indentation in the center.

The DeRenne name seems to originate with a man named George Wymberley Jones. He legally adopted the surname in 1866. This change solved the problem of misdirected mail meant for him or his (Jones) relatives. It also gave him and his family a certain élan in Europe, where his children were educated and he traveled. As a small addendum to the Girl Scouts, the attending physician at Juliette Low's death had an apartment in this building.

This entry looks more like a place from a bigger city, perhaps New York, or even Paris or London. The cold granite fenced courtyard seems to leave behind the Southern warmth of the walled gardens constructed in the preceding century. But for me it also calls to mind prehistoric temples such as Stonehenge, where the massive gray square-cut columns in the shadows set off the sun-kissed door like an altar-stone at an equinox.

8.

St. Vincent's Catholic School Side Gate

St. Vincent's Catholic School
Liberty Street

Gates of Savannah

The gate features a lacy, elaborate pattern and is surmounted by a high cross, with smaller crosses as details. Motifs include seashells and waves, symbols of baptism and grace. Mary, Star of the Sea, and Mary as Gate of Heaven are both titles of the Virgin from her litany. Other images depicted in the ironwork are the mystical rose, or Rose of Sharon, and the fleur-de-lis. The fleur-de-lis as a Marian symbol depicts the iris and sword lily, representing the purity of Mary and her sorrows. This decorative element is a repeated pattern in the Saint Vincent's gate.

–Sister Frances Ann Cook

The Convent and Academy of St. Vincent de Paul was begun in 1845 by Sisters of Mercy from Charleston, South Carolina, under the guidance of Mother Vincent Mahoney. The school building was designed in the Greek Revival style by Charles B. Cluskey. The original multitask, this property was a boarding school, orphanage day school and free school. It became an independent motherhouse a short two years later, and from here over twenty hospitals, schools and orphanages grew to serve the needs of Georgians throughout the state.

The Sisters of Mercy were noted and fearless in their dedication to treating the victims of yellow fever as well as the injured and dying of the Civil War, far above and beyond their regular duties.

9.

Sorrel-Weed Garden Gate

Garden adjoining residence and
bed-and-breakfast on the corner of
Bull and Harris Streets
Gate fronting Bull Street

Gates of Savannah

Built in 1840, this was the first structure erected on Madison Square. It was designed by architect Charles Cluskey in the Greek Revival style, and painted in a striking orange and rust tone. The Sorrel-Weed House is unique in Savannah for the symmetry of its four porches. The east and west porches are in horizontal balance, and the rear porches also balance vertically. Both General William T. Sherman and General Robert E. Lee guested here.

While I was painting, this house was undergoing renovations. In the process, the new owner had discovered a box inside a false ceiling with, according to the History Channel, authentic original Civil War surrender papers signed by General Lee. Supposedly, thirteen copies were distributed and only five known copies remain in existence.

I prefer to paint the look of the layers of peeling paint on the wrought iron, hinting at the years of changing owners and architectural trends. It is a gate without a section to close out the world, and as such, bears uniqueness and charm.

In 1939 the Sorrel-Weed House was recognized by the Historic Savannah Foundation. Later, in 1953, it was one of the first homes in Georgia designated as a state landmark. It is also a National Trust landmark.

The house is included on standard walking tours as well as ghost tours. As for the latter, it has been featured on several television shows exploring ghosts and other things that go bump in the night (notably the season finale of the Sci-Fi Channel's *Ghost Hunters*). Southern superstition suggests that certain hues brushed onto a porch roof will confuse ghosts, keeping them from entering and bothering the inhabitants. Evidently, the traces of the original haint (derived from the word haunt) blue paint on the upper rear porch stucco ceiling didn't do much good here.

10.

Double Courtyard Gate

Double gates connecting garden between
108 and 112 East Harris Street

Gates of Savannah

Variety is the spice of life, and this is an interesting departure from the plethora of iron gates. I enjoyed the way the scooped out wooden gate frames and echoes the back archway (with person-sized gate). The distant gate is crafted of the twisted wire that is the predecessor to our chain-link fences. These wooden double gates are more closely related to the large carriage doors that are still visible on the sides of some of the large old commercial buildings closer to the river.

The property at 112 was built for Wallace Cummings in 1857 and currently is divided into apartments; while 108 is a relative newcomer and a private residence, circa 1900.

Visitors and residents of Savannah will note that the background has been altered. There is a hint of a building, and then, it just appears to be hazy clouds. In reality, there is a monstrously ugly sky rise (Drayton Towers) behind that reflects the surroundings in alternating strips of glass between strips of concrete. Please excuse the judicial use of my artistic license. Let's just say it was a *really* hazy Savannah summer day—one that draws a gauzy curtain within a block of the sightseer!

11.

Green-Meldrim Side Gate

Green-Meldrim House,
1 West Macon Street
West of Madison Square,
south of East Harris Street

Gates of Savannah

This residence was designed by New York architect John Norris and built in 1850 for cotton merchant Charles Green. At a cost of $93,000, this Gothic Revival wonder features a crenellated roof and a porch embellished with filigree ironwork. Much of the material for the construction was brought over from England as ballast on Mr. Green's trading vessels, demonstrating some of the canny planning that helped him become rich enough to afford this mansion. The inside is also opulently decorated with marble mantels—including two in the drawing room of Carrara marble—as well as carved black walnut woodwork and doorknobs and hinges of either silver plate or porcelain.

The house was General William Tecumseh Sherman's personal headquarters during the 1864 occupation of Savannah. It was from here the general sent President Lincoln a telegram offering the president the city of Savannah as a Christmas gift.

The house changed hands in 1892 to Judge Peter Meldrim, who added the upper section to the gate and fence. The building was later sold by his heirs to St. John's Episcopal Church to use as a parish house.

According to Martha Summerell, the lower Gothic part of the gate and fencing are original to the house. The upper section was welded on from a later stock design.

Merana
Cadorette
©2005

12.

First Girl Scout Headquarters Side Gate

Building on 330 Drayton Street
Gate on East Macon Street

Gates of Savannah

Originally a carriage house built in 1848 for Andrew Low, this building had sheltered slaves, servants, horses, carriages, cars and miscellaneous other tenants prior to Juliette Gordon Low's investment in it as the first Girl Scout Headquarters, a gathering place for staff, meetings and tea parties, beginning in 1912.

Upon her death in 1927, most of the building was left to Savannah Girl Scouts to continue using with the exception of one side to be used as a garage for the Low house. By the late 1930s, Low's cousin, Nina Pape, had succeeded in lobbying for a "shrine" to remember Juliette on the property. Thanks to an exchange with the Colonial Dames, Savannah Girl Scouts could now claim the entire building. The addition, formerly owned by the National Society of the Colonial Dames of America, was to be transformed into the first Girl Scout museum.

A number of obstacles had to be handled. An ugly sliding door was slated to be removed, and this side gate was proposed. Due to wartime building constraints, however, a government board had to approve all requests. The mayor of Savannah sent a letter backing the Girl Scouts for permission and materials.

This Juliette Low gate was built in 1942. It originally had a wooden gate, which is still in use on the enclosure, hiding the air conditioner. On top was a lamp with a heavy iron base, which is housed in the archives until it is deemed safe to reinstall.

The building was left to the Girl Scouts of Savannah and has been in continual use for Girl Scouts ever since, longer than any other Girl Scout site in the United States. Currently, the property is open to the public, containing council archives, a museum, a program center and a shop.

13.

Andrew Low Front Gate

Museum and gate on
329 Abercorn Street

Gates of Savannah

The Andrew Low House was designed in 1847 by John Norris in the Italianate style. It fronts on the Southwest Trust lot near Lafayette Square. In colonial times, a jail stood on this site.

While the house was under construction, Andrew Low II's wife, Sarah Celia Hunter, his four-year-old son and his uncle died. Andrew inherited a vast estate from his uncle. In late 1849, a grieving but wealthy Andrew Low and his two daughters took up residence. Five years later, he remarried Mary Cowper Stiles, who graced him with three more daughters and a son named William Mackey Low.

Many famous individuals visited the influential Low family, including General Robert E. Lee and William Makepeace Thackeray. However, Girl Scouts hold it dear as the property bestowed by Andrew to their founder, Juliette Gordon Low, and her husband, William Low, upon their marriage in 1886.

Juliette Low often said she spent the happiest year of her married life here as a newlywed. Although most of their time (especially during the summers) was spent in England and traveling, this was home. She loved animals, and was known to stop and pet the cast-iron lions for luck on her way in or out. She left the carriage house adjacent to this to Girl Scouts of Savannah.

Low died here in 1927. The property has been owned and run as a museum since 1952 by the National Society of the Colonial Dames of America in the State of Georgia.

14.

Sunflower Front Entry Gate

Gate on 345 Habersham Street
Private residence

Gates of Savannah

I walked by this one several times before the lighting was right for me. The early morning sun just tops the home on the opposite side of the street to dapple the brickwork and highlight the wrought iron. The trick to painting this was accenting the black gate to make it stand out from the black door behind it. This was the first of the current naturalistic gates to be created in Savannah, and it caused a great stir. Locals still remember the many news stories and the few naysayers that thought it contaminated the historic district by veering away from the "traditional" style.

This gate was not the original main entrance. When built for John Kenney, the address was 319 East Charlton Street. The stucco was removed from the brickwork and the main entrance altered to Habersham Street in 1870.

This gate was crafted by Ivan Bailey, who operated Bailey's Forge from 1973 to 1982. He commented,

When I got the commission to make the first sunflower gates on Habersham Street, I puzzled for days trying to figure out what on earth I could do in such tall narrow spaces. One afternoon driving down Price Street, I saw a single lonely sunflower in bloom amid the tumbledown frame houses south of or around Waldburg Street and it suddenly hit me that this would be perfect.

It was my first gate commission. I wanted to sign it so I sat down and figured out how I wanted to sign things from then on. I've signed all but a couple pieces that way. It is I·B·MON·07. The dots are not on the baseline, but raised to the middle of the letter. The third element is the place name, now Monticello.

15.

Pineapple Courtyard Gate

Gate on 204 East Jones Street
Private residence

Gates of Savannah

This gate was built in 1860 for Abraham Minis and designed by Stephen Decatur Button. It is a very elegant gate with the traditional sign of hospitality crowning its columns. This opens into a lovely little formal grassed courtyard.

The pineapple is famous as a colonial symbol of hospitality. Its rarity, cost and unique appearance made it the crown of the most important meals. It was generally presented on pedestals above the rest of the fruits and desserts, just as architecturally it towers above the pediments of doorways and columns of gateposts. It was the ultimate symbol of hospitality whether presented to eat or crafted in a variety of materials to welcome the guest.

Located across East Jones Street is the well-known Savannah diner Clary's. In its past life, it was a pharmacy with a soda fountain and now has ties to *Midnight in the Garden of Good and Evil*. It has been a local gathering spot for over one hundred years.

16.

Garden Gate

Residence and antique store on the
corner of Jones and Lincoln Streets
Garden gate fronts Jones Street

Gates of Savannah

This property was originally built in 1856 and passed through a number of hands until it was refurbished and the gardens added by its present owner, James Morton. Morton actually reinvented, designed and now maintains this garden, reclaiming a vacant lot adjacent to the home and shop (although he prefers the word messuage, an old Anglo-French term for a walled compound). The property appears as if it has existed untouched by the passing years, which remains a tribute to his passion and commitment to horticulture and detail.

Morton has traveled extensively and often visited gardens, assiduously noting plants he found interesting or designs he enjoyed. This small area looks misleadingly large, due to his careful and thoughtful design, which also showcases his collection of antique English and European garden furniture and decorative items. A stone and brick path meanders through bonsai and statues of cherubs. A topiary compass lies centered in the garden. Directly inside the gate from the street, an old mill stone is used as a focal entry point.

Through this deceptively simple gate on this less-traveled side street have passed actors such as Julia Roberts, Madeline Stowe, Dennis Quaid and John Travolta, all of whom were filmed on this location at various times.

17.

Keep Out Courtyard Gate

321–323 East Jones Street
Private residence

Gates of Savannah

This residence was built for Mrs. Sarah Bailey in 1854. It is a very elegant, but literally over-the-top, exclamation of "Keep out!" This is one of the few gated enclosures I've seen in Savannah with an ironwork extension mounted on top, with a shorter version on the side yard.

At the time I was in Savannah, this duplex was beginning to be renovated, and the area behind this gate was a demolished mess torn up and full of construction debris. Current passersby who brave the formidable ironwork to peek through may see it restored. Instead of the variegated mineral seepings in my watercolor, the wall and home have been painted in a uniform yellow and are being marketed as condos.

Jones Street is one of my favorite walks overall. Start at either end and stroll across town enjoying all the restored elegance. Virtually the entire length is tree-lined, sometimes even canopied. Residential and all modern traffic sounds are a bit more muted. But watch your step wherever you walk in Savannah, as the pavement is very uneven and shifts in a bewildering lack of order. Individual property owners often seem to be responsible for their section of public walkway, so some sections may be level modern brick, abutting old shell concrete, onto frost-heaved stone flagging then onto mismatched two-hundred-year-old brick. Curbs can be almost flush with street pavement levels, or be a precipice to a foot-deep moat between sidewalk and street.

18.

Antiques Business Entry Gate

Business and gate on
12 East Taylor Street

Gates of Savannah

The property is the Thomas-Levy House, built in 1867, remodeled in 1896 into Second Empire Baroque style. As with many buildings in Savannah, the residence is above with a business on street level.

A simple side gate leads into the narrow passage between two buildings. After I had completed the watercolor, I stopped by to speak with the owners. To my pleasant surprise, I discovered they not only owned the property, but also had designed the gate themselves, salvaging bits of antique ironwork.

The final assemblage—constructed by Virginia and John Duncan around 1974—is so well done it appears perfectly suited to the time the home was built over one hundred years before. I like the casting work and built-in flower boxes, in which the blossoms change seasonally. The couple currently owns and runs V&J Duncan Antiques, which sells maps, prints and books from this location.

19.

Camellia Driveway Gate

Building on 426 Abercorn Street
Gate around the corner
on East Wayne Street

Gates of Savannah

This gate designed by Murray Galin in memory of Emmanuel Kronstadt an avid camellia enthusiast sculpted by John Boyd Smith Savannah GA

1987–1988

From a plaque posted on brick column beside gate.

During the early nineteenth century, camellias were one of the most prominent plants in Southern gardens. Brilliantly colored camellias nestled in dark green leaves brighten up the cold in Savannah from late January though March.

This is currently a private residence, originally built in 1855. It is an example of how modern smiths and designers have reinterpreted the gate as a sculptural rather than a geometric item.

This is one of several new gates in the area with a floral design. The gate's creator, John Boyd Smith, has a mechanical engineering degree from Georgia Institute of Technology, but was more inspired by the discovery of a set of blacksmithing tools in an old shed from his great-great-great-grandfather, master gunsmith Patrick Hoy. Since then, he has accumulated several awards, including some on the international level. While I have only three of Smith's gates included in this book, there are several others throughout the historic district, and in 1988 the Historic Savannah Foundation honored him for enhancing the area. His work extends beyond gates to other ironwork including functional items such as stair rails, entryways and furniture. Currently, he is also spreading out into some lovely non-functional sculptures.

20.

Gaslight Courtyard and Garden Gate

Gate between 15 and 19 East Gordon Street
Private residence

Number 19 was built in 1879, and number 15 was built for Charles McGill in 1854. The garden appears to belong to 19.

Mutual Gas-Light Company supplied the city until it was absorbed into the Atlanta Gas Light Company in 1875. You can spot several other lamps, most famously, on the façade of the Marshall House on Broughton Street. It is a gate that is different from many others, with the eternal flame shining above.

In the controlled jungle beyond the gate, there seems to be an infinite variety of shades of green. Tucked way in the back is a carriage house, barely visible through the greenery.

The gas lantern design seems fairly common to the period in which it was built. I have seen several around Savannah suspended on porches. The delicate lacy fretwork on top belies the large size of the piece.

21.

Little House Courtyard and Garden Gate

107 East Gordon Street

ARCHITECO...
THE LITTLE HOUSE
108 East

Mohana
©2006

Gates of Savannah

This is another of the modern, naturalistic gates built by John Boyd Smith, known locally as "Johnny the Blacksmith."

The main structure of the Little House was built for James Russell in 1856, and the north wing was added in the 1930s. The building houses Cowart Coleman Group, which specializes in Southern architecture.

The following information was provided by Sally Cowart of the Cowart Coleman Group.

> *The back part of our building was a carriage house, built in 1854. We found horseshoes under the floor during our renovation in 1999. The brick around the front ornamental gate is Old Savannah Gray Brick. Our building had been used as a gift shop for over sixty years before we bought it in 1999. We wanted the gate to resemble the leaf of the sycamore tree in our Little House garden. The gate was built and designed by local Savannah artist-craftsman John Boyd Smith for our office, Cowart Coleman Group Architects. The gate at our office entrance on Gordon Street welcomes everyone into our garden and our architectural firm.*

"Iron has a will of its own," blacksmith John Boyd Smith comments. "To manipulate it, you have to be even more strong-willed."

His wife, award-winning artist Rhonda Fleming, collaborates on the design concepts. Each gate then progresses to old-fashioned hammer and forge work, culminating in a piece of durable, functional artwork.

22.

"Skull" Garden Gate

Garden adjoining
115 East Gordon Street
Private residence

Gates of Savannah

This residence was built for Adolphus Gomm in 1869. No matter how many times I walk by this, and whatever the lighting, the little iron decorations at the intersections look like little skulls to me. Up close, the "nose" area is a flower, and the upper sides of the cranium are book-matched leaves curling inward.

The current owner, Mrs. Virginia Maxwell, maintained that it is not just morbid imagination to imagine the skulls. The fence's design was common in the nineteenth century, available as a catalogue item called "rosebuds." She suggests the design may have been used around cemeteries, possibly Laurel Grove. This fence was procured from its past use around Forsyth Park.

It is not surprising if surrounding a graveyard was the original intent, after seeing many of the creations decorating tombstones in the past. With high infant mortality, yellow fever and other diseases, our ancestors were much more familiar with death, and more accepting of it as part of everyday life.

23.

Hibiscus and Hummingbirds Garden Gate

Garden adjoining
313 East Gordon Street
Private residence

Gates of Savannah

This residence was built by Henri Hermann in 1861. The gate is yet another of John Smith's marvelous natural creations, commissioned along with a rear gate by Mr. and Mrs. William Bradley about twenty years ago.

I work from digital images, but frequently go back to check up and sketch elusive details. In this case, the reference shot I used showed only an outline of the pots and shadows of round orbs toward the tops due to the strong light and shadow contrasts. My best guess from this suggested a tiki-style container! Knowing that had to be wrong, I went back and found the "eyes" were radishes or turnips, and the nose and nostrils was a rabbit's head and eyes.

The owners are descended from the founders of Bradley Lock & Key Shop over on East State Street. It is an old-fashioned shop with a layout of keys in the pavement in front of the door, and old advertising slogans on the walls and over the side parking.

24.

Wheel Courtyard Gate

Corner of 102 East Gaston
and 444 Drayton Streets
Gate fronts on Drayton
Private residence

Gates of Savannah

This is a relative newcomer to the historic district, as it was built in 1928. The façade is drab, dreary, gray stucco relieved mainly by the side garden. Sheltered by the house on Drayton, the carriage house out back and an enclosed hallway connecting the pair, it boasts an abundance of blooms. Looking at the rays of the sunlight sparkling off the flowers and hedges through the outline of the wrought iron recalls the glow of stained-glass windows. There is a similar gate on the front right-hand side of the home on East Gaston Street, which is merely a path through shrubbery.

The wheel in the top panel appears a few other places about town, not only in gates, but as a protection to a few round ground-floor windows. Although in this painting the gate appears tall and the columns are fairly substantial, it is strictly the angle from where I worked. In reality, it is a friendly human-scaled entrance into a well-proportioned, sun-kissed sanctuary.

25.

Pink Front Gate

20 West Gaston Street
Private residence

Gates of Savannah

This home was built for William F. Brantley from a John Norris design in 1857 in the Italianate style. The property is also known for having one of the largest carriage houses in the historic area.

The iron lozenge pattern of the fence has become a well-used design for tourist items representing Savannah. I have seen it incorporated into various pieces of jewelry, photos, graphics, cards and bookmarks. The wheel symbol is a standard theme as well. This gate is on the northwest corner of Forsyth Park, the first large park created in Savannah, aside from the squares.

The park was influenced by the mid-1850s French trend of broad boulevards and parks designed to improve cities by way of making new industrial needs (i.e., access to the new railway stations, piped water and storm sewers and important public buildings) coexist with people's needs for fresh air, green space and comfortable middle-class and working-class suburbs. With all the wealth that cotton brought into Savannah in the 1850s, it is not surprising that city magnates chose to enhance and expand Oglethorpe's original plan. Bull Street became a promenade stretching all the way from the Exchange to the fountain.

Various historic markers may be found on façades, but most of the final locations on this tour are private homes. If you have a scholarly bent and want to delve into more information, the Historic Savannah Foundation is located at 321 East York Street. This particular home is just across the street from the Georgia Historical Society on 501 Whitaker Street.

26.

December Twilight Front Gate

26 East Gaston Street
Private residence

Gates of Savannah

This turn-of-the-century home was built for Mills B. Lane in 1909 from a design by Mowbray and Uffinger. Additions were made in 1926. *Savannah* magazine featured this home in an article in 2004. It has been extensively updated, but keeps all its vintage Southern charm.

A casual stroll from Gaston Street southward leads you into Forsyth Park. Walk to the center to catch the often photographed and painted fountain (created in 1858 and restored in 1988), which seems to appear in some form and almost every possible media in all local gift shops. Some of the fountain's restoration work was done in 1974 and 1977 by Ivan Bailey, who created a couple of the gates in this guide.

The last rays of the setting sun catch the top of the gate and lend it warmth against the dark door. We strolled by three nights before catching the right balance for this painting. It nicely ends my series of gates, as it celebrates the end of a season and year in an elegant glow as twilight deepens.

Although this is the last place I list, don't let that stop you. Every tour, whether by bus, trolley, foot or romantic carriage, has a different twist on the facts and frivolities that are Savannah. Thank you for joining me for an artist's walking tour and watercolor paean to a lovely city full of gracious people.

About the Author

Merana Cadorette has loved art since finding her first crayon. Her first commission was at sixteen, and her first major competition prize was won at eighteen. Between then and now, she has been happily married for almost thirty years, moved a dozen times, raised two children, been active in a number of volunteer organizations (especially Girl Scouting), earned he degree, been a guest lecturer and helped build tw houses, a barn and a hangar.

If you have a special attachment to any of thes gates, matted prints are available. They are offered i a standard size for ease of framing. Five-by-seven-in cards are currently offered in a limited choice of gat ("December Twilight" and the Girl Scout locatior Others may be added if enough requests are made.

Pricing and ordering information is available on Merana's website www.merana.com.

You also can mail comments or questions to:
Merana's Online Art Gallery
PO Box 690445, Vero Beach, FL 32969-0445